Winning Through Diversity

A Creative Approach for
Your Creative Success!

Marj Penley

Almanor Mountain High Press

Almanor Mountain High Press

ISBN 978-1-7343581-0-0

Dedication

To all creative folks everywhere!

How to Use This Journal

You will want to read over the beginning pages in which you will find a description of subpersonalities, a method for recognizing them as well as methods for directing and controlling them.

Next you will find a list of the stages most people encounter in their creative process. As you read about the stages, you might realize that the incubation stage does not apply to your particular creative work. That is, your work doesn't need an incubation stage. So, if that's the case, you can skip that page in your journal work.

Then, of course, you will want to experience your inner observer and director. You will find an exercise for doing that on the pages entitled, "Exercise for Observer and Director".

Now you are ready to begin to use this journal as you proceed through the process of your creative work!

You will have all the pages you need to explore and experience and direct your subpersonalities as you create your next creative project.

What Are Subpersonalities?

Although we like to think of ourselves as the same person all the time, we need to recognize the diversity within our unity.

We express different aspects of ourselves at different times.

The aspect we are expressing now is not the same one that was there an hour ago. When we're competing in our favorite sport, we may be very active and high achievers; at home watching a day of re-runs on TV, we are couch potatoes.

Furthermore, different people can bring out different aspects of us. For example, certain people tend to evoke our inner child selves. When we are around them, we may feel helpless, vulnerable or inadequate.

More on Subpersonalities

With our mothers, we may be childlike whether we're 3 or 33. When we watch a performance of Pavarotti or a recorded performance of Nureyev, we might experience the part of ourselves that appreciates beauty in music or dance--a sensitive or aesthetic self.

____

____

____

____

____

____

____

The Value of Subpersonality Work

The phrase 'divide and conquer' comes to mind.

Often, in our creative work, we don't know what is causing a problem for us or we don't know what to do next. We are inclined to think it is 'just us'. "We're stuck" or "we're not talented."

However, when we focus on our subpersonalities , we can discover those parts of ourselves that encourage and support our creative work as well as those that undermine it.

____

____

____

____

____

____

____

More on the Value

For example, instead of feeling discouraged with our work, we may recognize the voice of a subpersonality. If we are painting, we might hear that voice saying, “You’re no Rembrandt or Van Gogh, why are you wasting your time with paints?” As we recognize that this subpersonality is definitely not supporting our creative efforts, we will want to lock him up or reduce his influence in some manner.

Of course, we also have parts that encourage and support our work. When we realize that we have a whole company of inner parts, we can recognize them as well as directing and controlling them. Our creative work will almost always improve as we focus on our subpersonalities!!

____

____

____

____

____

____

____

How Best to Work with Our Subpersonalities

While there is much benefit from recognizing and naming a subpersonality,a person will usually gain the most if he or she is willing to work with them. Here are just a few ways that we can work with our subpersonalities:

1. When we don’t want or need a subpersonality at a particular time, we can contain it. We can put it in a closed jar or box, lock it in a closet, or put it in a yard enclosed by a fence or wall. Any type of imprisonment will do. (smile)

2. We can increase or decrease the size of the subpersonality. If we increase the size, we increase the influence or effect of the subpersonality. The reverse happens when we decrease its size.

3. We can turn up or lower the sound that the subpersonality makes. We can turn it off completely if we want.

More Ways to Work with Our Subpersonalities

4. We can imagine the subpersonality to be far away from us—or bring it up closer.

5. We can change the shape of the subpersonality.

For example, a shape with lots of sharp edges can be changed to one with curves.

6. If we allow an animal to represent the subpersonality, we can change the subpersonality by changing the animal.

For example, a timid mouse can be changed to a roaring lion.

____

____

____

____

____

____

____

How Can We Get to Know Our Subpersonalities?

The "Who Am I?" technique is an excellent method for meeting your subpersonalities.

Meeting your subpersonalities in this way is a little like going to a party where you don't know many of the people and you go from person to person, asking, "Who are you?"

You listen for a name and maybe some other fact such as the person's occupation or home town. "I'm Louise. I'm an attorney from Washington DC."

____

____

____

____

____

____

____

CREATIVITY EXERCISES

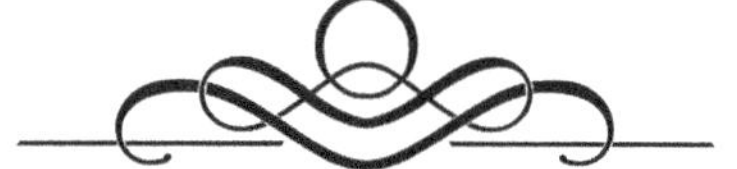

"Who Am I" Exercise #1

Select a place where you can be quiet and undisturbed. Take a workbook or journal and write the date at the top, and give it the title, "Who Am I?"

Then write your answers to this question. List as many of your subpersonalities as you can think of at the time, allowing your mind freedom to wander and wonder and roam, discovering many subpersonalities.

For example, in my imagination, I might see a woman giving excellent advice and I might name her the Wise Woman or I might see an ugly, old woman and I would name her a Hag. Then my answers might be: I am a Wise Woman, a Hag, an Earth Mother and so on.

____

____

____

____

____

____

____

My Subpersonalities

Name: ______________________________

Description: ______________________________

____

____

Name: ______________________________

Description: ______________________________

____

____

Name: ______________________________

Description: ______________________________

____

____

My Subpersonalities

Name: ____

Description: ____

____

____

Name: ____

Description: ____

____

____

Name: ____

Description: ____

____

____

"Who Am I" Exercise #2

Sit in a relaxed position. Close your eyes. Let your mind be clear like a blank screen. Then ask yourself again, "Who Am I?" and this time look for the answer in the form of an image on the screen of your mind.

Do not try to control or direct the images. Simply look for the images one at a time, and write down whatever you see, giving as much detail or information as possible.

One person wrote, "I am a mollusk without a shell, extremely sensitive to criticism and rejection."

____

____

____

____

____

____

____

My Subpersonalities

Name: ______________________________
Description: ______________________________
____
____

Name: ______________________________
Description: ______________________________
____
____

Name: ______________________________
Description: ______________________________
____
____

My Subpersonalities

Name: ____

Description: ______________________________________

____

____

Name: ____

Description: ______________________________________

____

____

Name: ____

Description: ______________________________________

____

____

"Who Am I" Exercise #3

Sit in a relaxed position at a table with your drawing pad or have your drawing pad in your lap.

Have some pencils, crayons or colored pens available. Pick up one of these and place your hands on the paper.

Then, with your eyes opened or closed, allow your hand to move up the paper in a spontaneous manner. You may find you scribble or doodle or make colored splashes.

Don't judge your work, but just allow your hand to make the responses to the question, "Who Am I?"

As we look at our scribbles, doodles and color splashes, we can imagine particular parts. A wavy line, for example, might suggest to us an indecisive subpersonality.

So when you finish with your drawings, you can look at them, using your imagination, and see what they represent to you. You'll probably discover several subpersonalities. If you like, you can name these subpersonalities or you can just leave them for now as the figures or forms on the tablet.

My Subpersonalities

Use the Space Below to Create Some Visual Images of Your Subpersonalities

My Subpersonalities

Use the Space Below to Create Some Visual Images of Your Subpersonalities

Observer and Director

To work with your subpersonalities, you will need to be able to disidentify--detach yourself from the subpersonalities.

The process requires the attitude of the observer. Now this observer simply observes and accepts. It does not condemn, discard, or eliminate.

The process also requires the attitude of a director who is detached from each of the subpersonalities.

____

____

____

____

____

____

____

Exercise for Observer and Director

To experience your observer as well as the director, do the following exercise:

Sit quietly and comfortably. Look around you and become aware of all that you see.

See it in all its detail, as clearly and as vividly as possible. Take a few moments to do this.

Now close your eyes, and breathe in slowly.

As you inhale, take in this vivid, visual awareness.

Then exhale and, as you do so, ask yourself "WHO IS AWARE?"

____

____

____

____

____

____

____

Exercise for Observer and Director

Still with your eyes closed, imagine that you are drawing a white circle with chalk on a blackboard.

Look at the circle. Be aware of it.

Then take a deep breath, and, as you exhale, ask yourself "WHO IS AWARE?"

____

____

____

____

____

____

____

Exercise for Observer and Director

Now let that circle fade away and, breathing rhythmically in and out as you have been doing, stay with the awareness of yourself as the one who is aware.

Really experience being yourself.

Try to get as clear a sense as possible of this experience. Take all the time you need to do this.

In this way you can experience yourself as the 'observer' and from this same place, experience yourself as the 'director', one who is detached from the subpersonalities and can direct the ones he wants to be on stage.

____

____

____

____

____

____

____

Stages in the Creative Process

In the following sections you'll find exercises that explore the stages of the creative process.

Here's a list of these stages.

- Decide on a Creative Project
- Start on Your Project
- Work on Your Project
- Incubate Your Work
- Work on Insights Gained from the Incubation
- Evaluate Your Work
- Complete Your Work
- Show Your Work

Identify Your Special Areas of Creativity

List ones you've been involved in or would like to be involved in.

Other Areas in Which You Are Creative

Add An Image of a Subpersonality

Decide on a Creative Project

What is the Creative Project
You Want to Focus on at This Time?

Subpersonalities on the Rise

In this very beginning, what subpersonalities come up for you? You will probably want to recognize and even list the subpersonalities that arise related to this very beginning--this decision to begin a particular creative project.

You will want to give each subpersonality a name as well as making an image of it with colored pens or pencils. (You can use the lined pages to describe the subpersonality in words and the blank page for your images.)

My Subpersonalities

Add An Image of a Subpersonality

Start on Your Project

Now you know your current creative project.

What subpersonalities come up for you as you focus on actually starting your creative project?

Remember you want to use the lined pages for the description in words and the blank page for the images or pictures of the subpersonalities

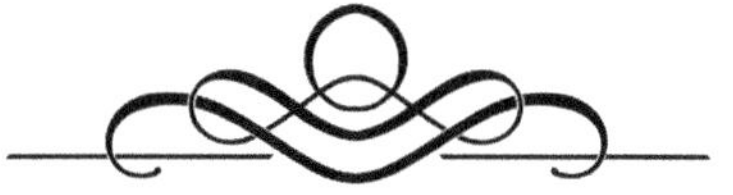

My Subpersonalities

My Subpersonalities

Add An Image of a Subpersonality

Work on Your Project

What subpersonalities came up for you as you began working?

Remember to use the lined pages for the description in words and the blank page for the images or pictures of the subpersonalities.

My Subpersonalities

My Subpersonalities

Add An Image of a Subpersonality

Incubate Your Work

If you have an incubation stage, what subpersonalities come up for you in this stage?

My Subpersonalities

My Subpersonalities

Add An Image of a Subpersonality

Work on Insights Gained from Incubation

What subpersonalities came up for you as you resumed work on your creative project?

My Subpersonalities

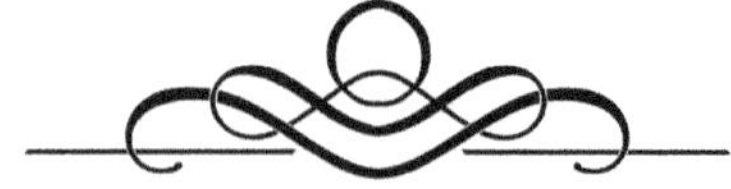

My Subpersonalities

Add An Image of Another Subpersonality

Evaluate Your Work

What subpersonalities come up for you at this stage?

My Subpersonalities

My Subpersonalities

Add An Image of a Subpersonality

Complete Your Work

What subpersonalities come up for you at this stage?

My Subpersonalities

My Subpersonalities

Add An Image of Another Subpersonality

Show Your Work

How about subpersonalities at this stage?
What ones show up?

My Subpersonalities

My Subpersonalities

Concluding Thoughts

Review of Your Subpersonality Work

Which subpersonalities are most helpful for your creative work?

What did you enjoy most about this Subpersonality approach?

Which subpersonalities seem to get in the way or sabotage your creative work?

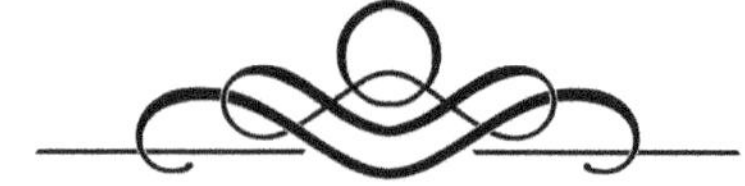

What methods have worked best for you to manage or control your subpersonalites?

Dear Reader

I would love to hear about your experiences in using this book, your creative process, and/or your creative life.

If you're curious about the classes I offer or the individual or group work I do, you are invited to get in touch:

Marj Penley
PO Box 820
Chester, CA 96020

Email: MarjPenley@gmail

About Marj

Marj (Marjorie) Penley, Licensed Marriage, Family Therapist, Certified Creativity Coach and ESL teacher (English as a second language) for over twenty- five years has been encouraging and supporting people all over the world to awaken, enrich and enhance their creativity.

With a large collection of techniques and procedures, Marj has facilitated the growth and development of many artists and writers.

Marj specializes in helping artists and authors learn to recognize and manage their subpersonalities. Focusing on subpersonalities has proven to be a delightful, engaging and unique approach.

Check out her website for testimonials
and more information: MarjPenley.com

www.ingramcontent.com/pod-product-compliance
Lightning Source LLC
LaVergne TN
LVHW050609100826
845148LV00015B/3200

* 9 7 8 1 7 3 4 3 5 8 1 0 0 *